Sweeping the Floors
in
The Full Crumb Cafe

Linda C. Anger

Dedication

This book is dedicated to any and all who have felt the pain, the joy, or the wonder of life and hurried to preserve it, mold it, or simply relive it.

This book is dedicated to those who encouraged me in my darkest times, and to those who told me I would "never earn a living as a writer."

This book is dedicated to my son, Ethan Flick, who puts the music of words to good use in his classroom, and to my grandchildren, Ava Alexandra Flick and Lincoln Michael Flick. Someday they will be old enough, I hope, to understand.

"Linda Anger's stories and poems read like excerpts from a complete woman's mind: some funny, some deeply disturbing. I laughed out loud at *House Call,* a story of shared secrets and maybe shared loneliness. *The Women of My Lineage* broke my heart: a sad poem, a true poem, an angry, outraged poem. So many others here that dare to challenge long accepted rules of being, laugh slyly at a middle-aged woman's moments of regret, or stand up to fight what can no longer be accepted."
—**Elizabeth Kane Buzzelli,** award-winning author of the Emily Kincaid Mystery Series (Midnight Ink)

"Linda Anger's wonderful poetry and prose delivers with an honest voice, one that does not hold back... you sense an inner strength that won't be shielded or compromised. Whether poetry or fiction, you'll believe everything Linda Anger tells you, and you'll want to read more." —**Diane DeCillis,** Author of *Strings Attached* (Wayne State University Press)

"*Sweeping the Floor in the Full Crumb Cafe* is poignant, imaginative and filled with surprises—everyday losses rendered vibrant and true. I enjoy Linda Anger's work immensely." —**Kelly Fordon**, author of *Garden for the Blind* (Wayne State University Press)

Linda Anger brings the voice of experience and a keen eye for detail to the ordinary moments that shape a woman's life, with a knack for turning midlife epiphanies into poetry. This delightful collection illuminates the tender topics we share with our most intimate friends, such as the handsome kid in the coffee shop who is way too young for us, and the things we do to comfort ourselves when our hearts are broken. —**Cindy La Ferle**, award-winning journalist and author of *Writing Home.*

"Some of these poems and stories of the people who pass through *The Full Crumb Cafe* have language so gripping, words and ideas so remarkable, that the reader can rest in their comfort even as the tension of the piece moves through them. Part bright fantasy, with splashes of terror and the possibility of freedom, this solid collection rests on the final, triumphant story of Cindy, the girl who never had a chance but made one for herself out of sheer determination. Is this collection a caper or a cautionary tale? I'd say in Anger's capable hands, it is both, and more."
—**Cynthia Harrison**, Author of the *Blue Heaven* series (Wild Rose Press)

"Linda Anger's poetry and short stories are rich, thought-provoking windows into situations that demand attention, inspire empathy and encourage looking beyond face-value. The best read I've had in a long time."—**Janice Rydzon,** Writer

Publication Credits

Mused: Bella Online Journal
The Space Between Now and Then (2013); *Boy in a Coffee Shop* (2014); *Iced Water with a Twist of Time* (2012)

Still Crazy Literary Magazine
The Women of my Lineage (2012); *House Call* (2013); *Apartment Laundry* (2015)

Michigan Prime Magazine (2013)
Hung up on Gordie Howe

Filthy Secret Books
I Might Have Chosen April (2012)

Plain View Press: Almost Touching (1996)
Dancer ; *The Afterlife of Roses*; *My Man can be so Irritating; Inheritance; Heroin; Reading Rumi; Duality; Night Visit; Menopause; Mama's Closet; Between the Leaves; Wallpapering;*

Contents

Acknowledgments

So many people have participated in my journey – some as helpers or guides, others as antagonists. I am grateful to all.

Special thanks to the women in my Detroit Working Writers critique group: Annick Hivert-Carthew, Debra Darvick, Diana Dinverno, Theresa Falzone, Cynthia Jalynski, Cindy LaFerle, and Iris Lee Underwood. You are gifted writers whose work I always enjoy. Thank you for your consistent support, editing advice, and encouragement.

My deep gratitude to M.L. Liebler, Elizabeth Buzzelli, Cindy LaFerle, Cynthia Harrison, Kelly Fordon, Theresa Falzone, and Janice Rydzon for reading and reviewing.

The Full Crumb Cafe

I go to the park down the street after dark, while the neighborhood children sleep, to sway on the old seesaw. Its weathered board, under layers of paint, carved initials and graffiti, has rocked three generations through life. I go there to sway in time and space, reel between history and possibility, work through an idea or problem, and to contemplate a metaphor: the teeter-totter of life.

In youth, my friends and I bounded back and forth, changing our minds, our perceptions and actions from moment to moment, rising headily to the top, falling to the bottom, and pushing off for the heights again. We were young and impetuous, failing to see the rhythmic wave that became a pattern, a map of our emotions and physicality. Our lives were measured only in extremes – good/bad, yes/no, light/dark, love/indifference; we had neither cause nor desire to consider the depth of our choices.

But later, when the games and gaiety of youthfulness eroded into careers, families, investments and responsibilities, our hearts and bodies began to ache; the patterns, then, became clear. We hungered for the middle ground, longed for the point on which the teeter-totter would balance and ceases to rock – the fulcrum of our hearts – where all was still, and non-action became the grit that would smooth our inner knowing, our inner depths. This space, and the elusive moments of clarity it brings, is the center of the Full Crumb Cafe – that halfway-between-the-worlds, metaphorical eatery, where we live, work, and play, making minute choices: whether to eat eggs or oatmeal, to speak harshly or stay silent, to hold tight or let go. Whether to cry or laugh like a Buddha, step out courageously, or walk away. We live here, work here, sleep here and love here – and pay our way as we go. The crumbs pile up beneath our chairs and tables, until we, or someone else, sweep them away.

There is something zen-like and vast about sweeping the floors in this place. Those who come here to eat, or to sweep, often leave much more than empty plates, dollops of butter or jam, crumpled paper napkins. They leave the scent of their thoughts, traces of their history, whispers of desire, and trails to their secrets.

We sweep under and around the chairs where they've sat, to remove table scraps and dust, of course, but also to clear the air for those who come next. We sweep the floors to keep tiny bits of granola or dust blown in from the street from crunching underfoot, and yes, to appease the health department.

But, there is more to our sweeping than physical cleanliness. There is intention, mindfulness of the gifts we gain in every interaction, whether we see and accept them or not, and awareness of the extraordinariness – the holiness – of engaging fully, honestly, and honorably in a simple task, an ordinary conversation, and all that they can teach us.

Those tiny bits of toast or pie that fall unnoticed from mouths and plates hold forgotten thoughts, unfulfilled desires. They are rich and nourishing leftovers – fragments of laughter, shards of anger, shadowy fears – and bright, electrifying moments of genius. When we sweep them together in the dustpan of our minds, they sigh, moan or giggle, spilling tales of extremes and motion, stories of insight, change and balance, stories of stagnation, transformation, despair and joy.

These are the stories of the Full Crumb Cafe.

Step In.

The door is always open.

The food is always fresh.

The teeter-totter has come to rest.

The Space Between Now And Then

One explosive morning you wake,
odd and changed,
in a foreign, unpopulated world
where nothing fits – not a single
shirt or pair of shoes, not your name
or the color of your favorite room.

Even your skin is alien,
and the face in the mirror vaguely altered.

One blazing morning you wake,
peculiar, mutated.
Familiar objects enlarge or shrink
in shape or shade,
walls and laws are immaterial.

Even the heat of thought
is transformed, exotic, unnerving.

One fiery morning you wake,
redefined, unchained –
and the chastising internal voices
that kept your life within the lines
are speaking gibberish.

Even the space between
now and then is blurred, inconsequential.

One searing morning you wake, discontent -
unplug the central heat of blind convention,
and re-ignite the embers in your hearth.

Dancer

I always wanted to be a dancer,
to step boldly in rhythms
of awareness, like a wraith,
to move lithely in both form and essence,
absorbed and changed
by a simple shift in cadence,
unfaltering in syncopated time,

to master the sultry samba
of lips on the verge of a kiss,
to sway with the waltz of hand-to-breast,
to immortalize in movement
the holiness of a single embrace,
transformed in the accent of a sigh,

to dip wide-eyed, allegro,
between hope and fear,
to welcome the adagio of solitude, dancing,
where even stillness becomes motion.

I Might Have Chosen April

Had the equinox fallen
on some other day,
and not ushered in the faintest
smell of autumn air —

had the dawn come before
I left my bed,
or the oak leaves not begun
to curl and darken,
had my neighbor's
maiden daughter not
worn a champagne
satin gown as she slipped
inside her white
stretch limousine —

I might have forgotten
the anniversary of my wedding,
and the chanting murmur
of discord that it veiled.

Had I known then
how quickly seasons change
and fragrance
fades from a bouquet,
the subtle shift from
hunger to disdain,
I might have chosen April,
and crossed my fingers
when I said "I Do."

Teen Idol

The girls scream and weep and
tug their hair, their barely-there
breasts saluting the gangly, gawky
man-child whose pants hang from his
bony ass like a boy on the down-low,
hand choreographed to his crotch
four times each song.

the girls sweat and swoon and worship,
in a fever they will never have for religion, moaning
"Oh,God!" as if he were one
instead of the industry-made
idol whose empty eyes betray the facade.

the girls flash their photophones and tell their friends,
"See - he smiled *right at me,*" pray he'll come at
night to be their boyfriend, hunger for the touch of his hand
down there, while all he wants is to go home and
be a normal boy.

Holding Back

Some women take a lover
When the days grow stiff or suffocating.
Some dive into sports or sports cars,
and zoom away with wind-pasted smiles
holding back their plaited hair.

Some women take a bottle
when the nights grow long or lonely.
Some go under therapy or underground,
and slip away with lofty hopes
holding back their resignation.

Some women take a pill
when the air is tense and unyielding.
Some head for a shop or chop heads,
and stomp away with rigid spines
holding back their humbled pride.

Some women take a class
when the world is cold and empty.
Some learn how to knit or nitpick,
and fade away with smoldering eyes
holding back their fiery tongues.

I pour peanuts in deep
earthenware bowls,
dress them in triple-chocolate fudge
ice cream, sink into the sofa,
and don't give a thought to holding back.

Rum Runner

Henry ran rum across the Detroit River,
his boat slow and low in the water.
Heavy with bootlegged bottles, he'd row alone,
fearful of detection,
but a nip or two was all it would take
to wash his fears away.

There were nights he'd chant seafaring songs,
halfway into the channel, halfway out of sobriety,
crossing the wake of freighters
coming down from Whitefish Bay.

There were nights he'd curse the radiance of the stars,
curse his pious wife and hungry children,
curse the ticker-tape and market shares
that caused the tidal wave
that drowned his simple world,
curse the flag, the land, the sea.

But he never did curse
the slippery warmth
of his rum wages
spilling down his throat.

We Kiss the Inside of our Men

Ordinary women sleep at night, content
with husband, home and family.
They settle for *the way it's supposed to be.*

For us, nothing is ever settled, only
a subterranean, volcanic rumble –
a buried, untamed knowing – eruption-on-the-verge.

Ordinary women live on the surface,
keeping their homes clean.
They wash and dust and put things straight.

For us, there is no proper place,
only temporary shelving, inside and out.
A tumultuous flow, a stone that rests
in river beds till washed downstream.

Ordinary women press hems, steam vegetables.
They bake and broil and tuck the sheets in tight.

We, gypsy squatters in claustrophobic cubicles –
we see raveled threads as omens,
broken hearts as prayers.

Without internal law or order,
without ropes and chains,
no ordinary women,
we hold the heat,

and kiss the inside of our men.

The Afterlife of Roses

Hannah brought flowers to every birth and death in the neighborhood. Her bouquet was always the same: a single red rose, a white carnation, and a sprig of ladyfern tied with a black satin ribbon.

The other children were afraid of her, the odd old woman at the end of the street. But I had seen enough of Hannah mending broken wings and growing lush garden beds in soil farmers had forsaken, to trust the gentle wisdom beneath her ancient, stern appearance. I alone would meet her eye through the foliage as I hop-scotched down the sidewalk with the other girls. I alone would journey into her yard and eventually her home, to learn things long forgotten yet still alive, things made of mystery yet more real than the earth under our feet.

When I was five, my cat tangled with a speeding car and lost. Hannah slopped through the hedge between our land and hers, to stand at dusk above the grave my father had dug for Buttercup's broken body. She spoke softly, then moved back through the hedge without bending a branch.

I could not see clearly in the dim light, but knew she had left something there. Weaving my way through the yard, pretending nonchalance, I came upon the grave only after fawning over flowerbeds, playing on the old rope-and-tire-swing, and finally arriving as if totally surprised to find myself there. She'd left a small bouquet – one perfect miniature rose, one white dwarf carnation, and one single sprig of ladyfern, tied with a black satin ribbon.

Her piercing, gentle gray eyes caught mine through the dark hedge, now flecked with fading daylight. Nothing moved as she spoke. "Release life back to itself, little one. Let go of your tears and your pet. Release him. Release yourself." I untied the satin knot. The flowers sprawled across the mound of dirt. Hannah drew a sharp, deep breath. "It is done," she whispered through the branches. My sorrow was gone. Hannah vanished from beyond the hedge.

From my room that night, I watched shadows dance in the flicker of candlelight through the curtains of her windows. My dreams were filled with strange, exotic plants and aromas. I walked old forest paths, woven – handed with Hannah. When morning came, I moved through the hedge without bending a branch.

Over the years, Hannah taught me everything she knew of gardening. We spent hours planting and mulching, pruning and aerating. Her yard was a maze of plots and pots. In time, I came to know the secret names and uses for hundreds of flowers and herbs. Hannah taught me to carefully slice all but one woody thorn from a rose stem, to steep petals and leaves for teas and medicines. I learned to gauge the passage of the season in the gentle unfolding of a rosebud, to welcome bees and earthworms as much as birds and butterflies.

It became my job to keep her informed of expectant mothers and impending deaths in our neighborhood. Together we would hunt out the perfect blossoms, tending them for days in anticipation of their carefully prepared function. Together we would label and store the ointments, salves, and tinctures she used to heal aching joints or broken hearts throughout the winter months, while the gardens rested under deep snow.

The ritual for a birthing was different than for a death, although the ingredients were the same. Hannah would arrive at a birthing with the pieces of her gift stored in separate pockets. She assembled the bouquet as she stood over the cradle, speaking so only the child could hear, and left immediately after her gifting was complete. The satin knot was left intact.

And so I passed from childhood to womanhood, tending gardens and neighbors with Hannah. Marriage and a house two hundred miles away made my trips home sporadic and far too short. Ten years passed before I went to visit for the summer.

Hannah and her gardens had grown sparse and dry. The vibrant dahlias of my youth were gone, the coreopsis beds taken over by weeds and wild grasses. Scarlet roses, dying on the stem, turned the color of old dried blood. White carnations were almost transparent, like the rice-paper skin stretched over her hands.

In her old bentwood rocker, which I'd move outside each morning, Hannah would watch as I cleared overgrown beds, planted health seeds and began to gather flowers. Within weeks, her gardens had returned to their earlier splendor. Despite her increasing frailty, Hannah was the most radiant I had seen her in decades.

I laughed when she gave me the hickory-twig broom her teacher had made a century earlier. I wept when she forced me to pack the journals of her recipes and procedures, begun when she was 13, for shipment to my home. Hannah died at midsummer, in her 95th year. I waited at the funeral home, but no one came. The street belonged to strangers now. My childhood friends and neighbors had long since moved away, or died themselves.

And when the minister had read his psalms and epistles, when the funeral director stood ready to extinguish the candles, I placed my bouquet over her heart – a single red rose, a white carnation, and a sprig of ladyfern, tied with a black satin ribbon. I spoke so only she could hear, repeating the words she'd taught me so many years ago:

> Red for the blood of woman,
> White for the seed of man,
> Green for the earth you walked upon,
> and Black for the mystery that binds them.

I untied the satin knot. The flowers sprawled across her breast, and I heard Hannah whisper, "It is done." My sorrow was gone.

My daughter, Hannah, was born the next spring. Last night, just five years old, she moved through the hedge without bending a branch.

The Women of My Lineage

The women of my lineage stand
starched and solemn-eyed
in tattered photographs without notation.

Mother pours stories of the family patriarchs
like bottles of vintage wine,
recalled with palatable, fluid detail.

Great Uncle Gideon fathered 13 children.
Two wives died in winter hunting camps,
and the last, sent sight unseen to
the Western Canadian woods
to darn socks and carry
river water. A stocky mail-order bride.

Her name is unknown.

Great-great-grandfather John's military record,
preserved and archived—
twice captured in the Civil War,
attached to Custer's army.

My sisters are not certain
if the bustled, buttoned matrons are
great-grandmothers, grand-aunts,
or unrelated faces, tossed carelessly
into the wooden box that came
from North Ontario a century ago.

The women of my lineage
are nameless, unheard voices,
mummified in patriarchal linens.

Stole and Tails

Refused entry at the door,
 we laughed our way home
in soggy jeans and
laceless sneakers,
down puddled April streets.

You, stuffed in a moth-holed
cutaway with fraying tails,
me, mummied up in some dead
flapper's fringed silk stole,
$2.50 each at the Salvation Army.

A strain to our budget, but
the invitation read:
Formal Attire Required

I Saw a Girl Today

for Janice, 2013

I saw a girl on the street today
and thought it might be you,
long, curly black hair flowing
down her back –

those rich, black curls I envied,
the thing you said branded you
as a Jew as clearly
as the tattered yellow star
stitched to your grandfather's coat
as he wandered the Warsaw ghetto.

I saw this girl, but before my aging legs
could spring into action to
chase you down,
I remembered it was 40
years ago when we were young like her:
You, so alive, almost brazen,
me, quiet, close to timid.

That was years before your love
affair with dangerous men and needles,
decades before that day last spring
you gave yourself an overdose so grand,
so intentional, it would have
killed you, your grandfather,
and even me, if I had known.

I saw a girl on the street today,
and wanted her to be you,
young, whole,
laughing with me.

My Brothers' Bones

Excavation, 2012, Rochester Michigan

Beneath the patched cellar floor
of the building at Third and Main,
my brothers' bones were found
in 1899, under cobblestones,
side by side, one head
pointed east, the other west.

People were amazed; everyone knew
Indian burial grounds were
two blocks north, along the old railway,
whose single-room depot
still stands, its tracks
torn up and tossed away.

The bones were "gathered up,"
the old newspaper said;
no one knows where they
were taken.

Now, men in hard hats
replace the road
and find my own bones,
a sidewalk's width
from where my brothers laid,
eight feet below the surface.

Of my age and ancestry
none can say, until
they find my brothers,
or a century from now, unearth
the lonely bones of others.

My Man Can Be So Irritating

I don't mean the wayward socks and shirts
that never make it to the hamper,

or bitter words that scorch my heart,
forgotten anniversaries, or unmowed lawns.

I have no profound insight on gender differences,
or the politics of why God is called *He* instead of *It*.

I'm referring to that numb redness
of my skin after we make love,

how his evening stubble rakes across my body,
leaving tiny rivers that fill with pain and pleasure

and tingle there for days.

Boy in a Coffee Shop

He's the boy
I would have loved
when love was still
within my reach.

Shoulder-length dark hair
in waves, not curls,
long sideburns,
clean-shaven,

Slender fingers meant
for guitar strings, piano keys,
or midnight massage,
faded jeans
and wide-set eyes.

He looks up and
past me,
beyond my silver hair and
crow's feet;
smiles at the girl behind me.

He looks up and
past me
while a chorus
of my dark-eyed ghosts
share his table,
still within my reach.

Recurrence

Don't tell me I "have to"
let you slice me again,
or believe I will be whole,
when the sadness in your

guarded eyes tell me you
don't. Tell me: "I will look
at the results once more,
just to be sure. Maybe

it's a false positive."
If I have no real hope,
don't tell me. I have two
choices: Ignore you all

and finish in God's time,
or embrace, without regret,
your toxic option. But
don't tell me I "have to."

House Call

I never believed in love at first sight, and I still don't. Love inside of a month? That, despite all the scientific training and personal development classes I've had in my life, is a different story— one to which I can attest.

Pete Simmons was a quiet guy most of the time, going about his business as an IT magician. You know the kind—the one that's called in when all else and everyone else, has failed to fix the problems or the crashes. He's the consummate geek—thick glasses he's worn forever—tried contacts once but was so accustomed to the frames he couldn't stop pushing at his nose even when the frames weren't there.

He comes in your house or office and struggles to say much more than "hello, and what's the problem?" then he asks you to leave the room because he needs to focus and can't do that if you're the type to ask a bunch of questions and he wouldn't talk to you anyway. A half hour later or maybe an hour, he comes out, says "all set, then," hands you a bill, and rocks nervously, heel to toe, while you write the check.

That's how I met him, actually – the day my 5-year-old desktop computer whirred and sputtered to a stop for the fifteenth time. My regular tech guy, Bruce, had told me a month earlier the old PC was "a goner," and he wouldn't be able to resuscitate it again. Gave me Pete's card, saying "If there's any life left in it, this guy will find it."

He wore faded jeans, a solid black t-shirt, those coke-bottle glasses, and laceless high-top sneakers. His hair was this nondescript color—mutt brown, my mother used to call it. Somewhere close to 6 foot tall, skinny as a proverbial rail, and nervous. Very nervous. He brought my PC back to life in less than ten minutes.

"Bruce says I should chuck it and buy something new," I said, hoping for solid advice from the man who was the guru to the gurus in the IT world. "Huh," Pete said, keeping his eyes on the screen.

"I just don't have the money, right now, ya know?" I said, pacing the room.

"Huh," Pete said, tapping the keyboard and slipping a disc in the CD drive.

"So waddaya think? Should I max out my one credit card and get a tablet?"

"Huh – uh, What?" He finally looked up at me as he stood up.

"Should I buy a new computer?" I asked.

"This one's working fine." He wrote out the bill at my kitchen counter.

"Well, yeah, but…"

"Call me if it crashes again," he said, walking out quickly as soon as I handed him the check.

And I did, exactly one month later.

Now I have to admit that I'm a geek, too, but not like Pete. I'm a science geek, a pathology technician, spending my days cutting thin slices of tissue and staring at them through a microscope looking for cellular abnormalities. I'm a cell geek. And when you spend hour after hour sitting at a microscope watching nothing but cells go by it feels pretty good to have someone to talk to when you get home. Pathology is not a terribly interactive profession.

But there's no one waiting for me at home, except my dog Fido. Yeah, that's really his name, not very creative, I know, but I inherited him from a shelter and they said "Fido" was the only name that caused him to lift up his head and wag his tail. So, "Fido" it stayed. He's good at tail wagging and slobbering on me, but he's not conversational.

So when someone – anyone – comes to my house to repair something, like the washer or the water heater, or in this case, my ancient PC, I can't help myself. I want to talk. I want to hear another human speaking back to me.

21

This one night—a month after the PC crash—I was almost hyper after work. I'd found a single cancer cell in a tissue sample. A single cancer cell that my lab partner on that shift had missed – every slide is checked by two technologists because the work is so delicate. My partner Jake, who works on a 10x binocular research microscope, said the slide was clean and went home for the day. I punched the slide into my brand-spankin' new trinocular research scope, pumped the magnification up to 100x and there it was – a single cell with raggedy edges, looking just about ready to duplicate. I snapped a photo with the built-in Ivu 3000 camera attachment, and in an email, sent the image of the cell to the emotionless chief pathologist who didn't want to spend the money for the new scope, and a copy to Jake.

It's pretty exciting when you realize you've saved a life just by looking in a microscope. I'm not kidding myself, I'm a technician, not a pathologist, but if I hadn't jacked up the magnification as high as it would go, that lady would be a walking time-bomb, strolling around not knowing that her one little cell was duplicating like crazy and turning into a tumor and blasting its clone cells all across her entire body.

So naturally, I wanted to share my discovery with someone. My neighbor Natalie wasn't home. My sister was in Europe with one of her fancy theatre groups. My last boyfriend, Spencer – well, no matter how bad I wanted to hear another voice, I wasn't about to call him.

So I called Pete.

"Computer's down again, can you come over?"

"Huh. Sure, be there in 20 minutes." He said.

I flipped on the PC, printed out the list of my latest Google search, then reached behind the desk to pull the electrical cord halfway out — just enough to cut the power without being obvious that this service call was a set-up. No battery life in this old girl, she needed to be plugged in to come alive.

"Hi Pete," I said as soon as he walked through the door. "Guess what? I saved a life today!"

"Huh," he said, walking past me to the small bedroom I'd converted into an office. The walls were lined with books like *Abnormal Cell Growth in Hormonally Deficient Children,* and *The Role of Differentiation in Tumor Growth.* The other books – the ones no one knew I had, the ones that would cause my colleagues at the lab to lose all respect for me – were in the file drawers of the desk.

Pete sat there, pressing keyboard combinations, trying to raise my PC from the dead. "Huh" was all he said when each attempt failed.

The phone rang; I headed into the kitchen to find my purse. Gary at the lab, calling to ask would I'd switch shifts tomorrow? Yeah, sure. Pete scooted out the door and was rifling around in his truck, probably looking for some part he thought was broken. I spent the next five minutes struggling to put the schedule changes in my smart phone calendar. Sometimes smart phones aren't so smart.

Next thing I know, Pete was standing in the kitchen doorway with a thick book in his hand. I recognized it immediately, it was one I'd read at least a dozen times so far, I felt the heat of embarrassment rising from my belly right up to my face. *True Life Alien Abductions in the 21st Century.*

"Where'd you find that, Pete?" I asked, snatching it from his hands.

"Huh. Found it fishing in a drawer for a paper clip. Have you read *My Day in a Spaceship?*"

"Uh, no," I replied, stunned that the secret passion I'd held for so many years, the research I'd been following for decades, might be of interest to a guy who was the consummate computer geek, and he'd just uttered an entire sentence, for god's sake.

"What kind of crazy story is that?" I finally asked, not sure if I was mistaken in his interest.

"You don't mean that, I already know," he said, taking a step closer. "I saw 'em all – all the books hidden in all the drawers in your office. You just like reading the books, or are you in it for real?"

"What? What do you mean, 'in it for real'?" I asked as he took another step closer and tilted his head down so that, for the first time, I got a good look at his eyes, magnified by his glasses. Grey, the color of sea water in a driving storm, with a sprinkle of cinnamon-colored rods. Strange. Beautiful. I was in love.

"Computer's fixed," he said, flashing a smile as he walked out the door. "No charge today. Call me when it happens again."

I watched him drive away, then headed to the office. The plug was snug in the outlet, the screen was bright and freshly cleaned, and a small thin book I didn't recognize was sitting face down on my desk chair.

My Day in a Spaceship: a Personal Story of Alien Technology. And there, in the lower right corner, was a photo of the author, Pete Simmons.

"Huh," was all I could say as I turned to page one.

Inheritance

In this old house, nothing is ever lost.
The murmurs of long-ago love talk,
the brown aroma of beef-barley soup,
the strains of a plaintive violin –
all cling to flocked wallpaper.

Secrets are dust on a shuttered window pane,
bootlegged whiskey in the cellar,
stolen chocolate from the five-and-dime,
a mistress on the other side of town.

Unfinished arguments, blue ribbon,
childhood sweethearts, black eyes
awake to slip from furniture and walls at night;
they are contented signs and soulful tremors.

Lives layer, passing eyes
and chins through generations,
china cups through tiers of grandmas;
bridal veils are tucked in scented tissue.

In this old house nothing every dies.
Shadows live in vaulted ceilings,
soak up the passing days,
and hold the walls together.

Heroin

All the kisses mamma withheld,
you say,
while your hollow eyes
search
for spoons and matches.

Better than any lover,
you say,
while your fumbling hands
prepare
another needle.

I'll check into rehab tomorrow morning,
you say,
while your veins bulge
under rubber tubing.

I know I'll stay clean this time,
you say,
but I'd die for one last fix tonight.

And you do,
a needle full of kisses
piercing the
whiteness of your
inner thigh,
where a lover
might have dreamt.

Reading Rumi

The Sufi Says:
When two unite in love or hate,
a spirit third is born.
These Beings live within the ethers,
have form, speech and vision.
They must be gently tended.

While scents of your body still
linger on my skin,
and voices of your seed still
echo in my womb,
you ask me to no longer breath you in, or listen.

Who will tend the spirit children we gave life?
They are fervent words, impassioned kisses,
churning in my belly.
Mirrors of loving and discord,
they do not know you've gone.

Wraith-like and hungry, they wail behind
my swollen eyes;
I strain to lay their shadows down,
but reach them only when I breath, or listen.

Two Robins Had Sex

this morning,
hooked together and
flapping like mad
ten inches above the
crooked rock
by the oak tree

and

when the flapping
was done
they shared a worm
that had come up
for an innocent stroll
through the dew

and

then the girl Robin
flew south
and the boy Robin
strutted to another
worm hole

and

neither one wanted
a second date

and

I was reminded
of you.

In the Gypsy Theatre

The stoic therapist says I'm looking for my father.
An Alexis Complex lived through an army of transient men.

Yet in the wings of this ancient theatre
come actors and staging of a different shape.
Curtains rise and fall, telling other stories,
less common and predictable.

I've never lived an ordinary life.

The gypsy wanders one town or the next,
holding to no roots or obligations. The gypsy sings,
low and rich; the townsmen shiver, the women stay inside.

They damn his loose-fit clothes, his cloak
of indifference to their laws and orders.
In him they see their own wanderlust,
the mournful wail of their shadowed longing.

I wear the boys and men who've graced my life like a colorful map.
They come to me hungry, these sons of fearful men;
they come to be fed, to dance with abandon, to sleep satisfied.

But solemn church bells call them home, to harness their feet in tight
leather boots, bury their shadows in laws and orders.

For some I cinch my waist with the belt of their belief,
bear sons and cook exotic foods – until the rise of a blazing moon,
when shoes grow tight and church bells ring in judgment.

In the wings of this ancient, warm theatre, actors and staging wax
and wane, curtains rise and fall.

I've never lived an ordinary life.

To Be Filled Again

Yesterday
Snow fell
From dense, low clouds
Racing southwest to northeast and
I felt the weight of
You
Falling from me.

Today
wispy grey
leftover clouds crept back,
northeast to southwest,
empty, pale,
Hungry

To be filled again.

Iced Water with a Twist of Time

This drink,
iced and purified,
once touched the lips of
Australopithecus Afarensis –
Lucy in her first bipedal steps –
3 million years ago in Ethiopia.

Drawn from lakes, released
from faucets, evaporated, rained,
recorded, invoked –
billions of gallons,
rivers of thought,
around and around
in endless recycle.

This same water was sipped
from Buddha's cupped hands
along the Ganges, cleansed wounds
on the beaches of Normandy,
fed cornfields in Kansas.

The quiet pond at my center
knows what Lucy knew;
the fluid touch and
illusion of time,
life's undertow and current.

Like water, I roll down crooked paths,
drop to the depths of myself
and swallow,
a ripple in liquid history.

Duality

Your demanding voice
on the phone
slices through me
like a rusty blade.

My belly thuds
like a stone
on damp earth,
unable to howl
leave me alone,

while you hear
only my soft
hello.

Little Boys in Old Men Bodies

Carts stacked
on the first tee,
The four old men in front,
handicapped flags on their carts,
stumbled to the ladies tee box,
too frail to hit from further back.

The one with wooden clubs
even older than him
hit high and long,
straight down the fairway.

"How does he do that?"
asks the one in checkered pants.
"He has a girlfriend with big tits,"
says the one in a cowboy hat.

"Ah, a girlfriend," they all nod.

Night Visit

I wake at night,
feel you curled against my spine.
I wrap myself in you.

I wake, aware it was not
a dream, but still,
it is a mystery.

I touch the place I thought you'd been.
Perhaps are. Again
I sleep, content.

Hung Up on Gordie Howe

At his heyday, the entire hockey-loving world – including my mother – was hung up on Gordie Howe.

Scotty Bowman, the most successful NHL Coach in history, loved Gordie because he could play center, right wing, and defense, and could shoot right or left-handed.

Mom loved Gordie for other reasons. They were both Canadians; they were the same age, even though she was three years older. Gordie was signed by the Detroit Red Wings at age 16, making his NHL debut with the Wings at age 18, the same year my American dad married my Canadian mom and brought her to Detroit.

Mom went on to raise five Red Wing fans, and Gordie went on to lead the Wings to four Stanley Cup championships, and to first place in regular season play for seven consecutive years. At the end of his career, he was a six-decade mega-superstar, called "Mr. Hockey," and the only player over which my mother swooned.

Gordie was 40 years old and still playing on the summer evening in 1968 when my parents drove off from our home in Orchard Lake to visit friends in Bloomfield Hills, leaving me and my sister, she aged 20, me 17, to tend to our 5 and 4 year-old siblings.

My father was a WWII Navy Pilot, downed in a crash that spared his life, but left scar tissue that continued to grow, slowly and silently on his brain, for the next two decades. On that night, 26 years after the crash, on a stretch of Long Lake Road in Bloomfield Hills with Mom in the passenger seat, he had a grand mal seizure.

Somehow Mom stopped that car, and ran to the closest house. She pounded on the door, which was quickly answered by a tall man with bright blue eyes and a familiar smile.

"Call an ambulance, my husband is… my husband is…OH MY GOD! YOU'RE GORDIE HOWE!" she cried. "I'm Canadian, too, and have loved you forever, and, and… I think my husband is dead in the car."

Meanwhile, back at the house, my sister and I were playing records really LOUD, and teaching our little siblings to paint Day-Glo peace signs on the bedroom walls.

I was the first to the ringing phone.

"Hello, this is Gordie Howe," the man said.

Now, I'm only seventeen, but I'm no fool. I know who Gordie Howe is, and, I know the odds of him calling our house on a Friday night in 1968 are about three zillion to none.

"Yeah, and my name's Tinkerbell," I say, slamming the receiver down.

"Some idiot pretending to be Gordie Howe," I tell my sister, as if we would be stupid enough to fall for something that absurd. We laughed and laughed until the phone rang again.

"Don't hang up!" the man said. "Were your parent's expected at the Carney's house?"

"Yyyyyyeeeeesss," I said. "Who is this?"

"This is Gordie Howe. Your father has been taken to the hospital. The Police need you to come get his car." He told me where they were and promised he would stay with the car until I got there.

I arrived to find EMTs and police officers talking to a tall, slender man in street clothes. The police wanted the car moved.

"I don't give a #$@% about the car," I said. "I'm going to the hospital. Where did they take my dad?"

The officer, a burly guy, was raising a chiding finger toward my face, when Gordie Howe, my mother's hero and at that moment my own, gently swept his hand away with the grace that can only come from a lifetime of precise hockey-sticking.

"Officer, I'll drive the car to your station," he said. "They can fetch it tomorrow."

At the hospital, I found Dad dazed, but alive, and Mom flushed by the anxiety of the situation, and the thrill of meeting her hockey hero. Dad was released a few days later, and all the bridge club ladies sympathized with her harrowing experience, and envied her soiree with the great Mr. Hockey.

Gordie called our house several times over the next weeks, to ask about Dad's progress. At Mom's request, he sent autographed photos to relatives in Canada and the bridge club ladies.

Mom never lost her affinity with Gordie, and still giggles when his name is mentioned.

And me? I'm probably the only woman in America who can say, "I *hung up* on Gordie Howe."

Exfoliating Eden

Chop down your fabled apple tree,
my love,
its ancient nectar will not
quench your thirst.

Bid farewell to Paradise,
my sweet,
and strip away its luscious
limbs and leaves.

Men walked there
with gods and snakes,
content to feed and sleep
without concern.

Women woke there,
reached through leafy shadows,
to savor the juice
of forbidden fruit.

But nothing springs from weary
roots, my pet,
or sprouts in barren sands,
and even tended fruit
is quickly spoiled.

Still, your epic hunger
grows — for apples,
apples, apples.

Menopause

Perhaps I fear my days grow shorter
as the moon deserts my womb,
or that my womanness will
bleed away, in dried-out joints
and fractured memory.

This decades-old regularity,
a rhythmic hinge on which
I plan weekends with a lover,
safe times to wear white trousers,
has grown erratic,
a discordant trickle that shifts
the contours of my breasts and spine,
shifts the cadence of my life.

No longer virile-wombed, not yet a barren crone,
but adrift between these worlds,
I've fallen out of tune with lunar cycles,
and hear my dead grandmothers
begin to call me home.

Mama's Closet

Mama hid everything in her walk-in closet, like the bag of marijuana and string bikini she found in my sister Nancy's purse. Of course, Nancy knew where to look – Mama never threw anything away. Her closet was stuffed with old lace dresses and feathered hats. Teddy bears and Christmas aprons crouched among shoes she had not worn in twenty years. Glass jars full of buttons from worn-out clothes blinked between papered hat-boxes.

I would sit on the deep shelf behind pastel crinolines, reading the stack of yellowed letters from somewhere in the South Pacific, or try to play Dad's bass drum with my tiny bare hands.

The scents and textures of past and present mingled there: a museum, a holding place for the unresolved difficulties of marriage and parenthood. As a child, I wondered why she saved all those useless things, why she put the things she took from our rooms in the one place she knew we would look.

Last week, I found a *Playboy* magazine under my son's mattress. I left it there. My closet is full enough, with bags of bell-bottom jeans, go-go boots, and a stack of yellowed letters from somewhere in Southeast Asia.

Foreign Tongues

I leave my tongue on the coffee table
next to your half-filled mug,
knowing you'll explore it
while I'm gone.

I envision your investigation,
hear you inquire as to
the oddity of dialect and cadence,
weigh it against the voices of your past,
and search for innuendoes.

Yes, I know that while you
have my tongue I cannot speak.
But what words would I say
that could be clearly heard
by anyone but you?

When I return,
I find it nestled
by your ear as you sleep.

And I know:
You've understood my language.
We are no longer speaking
foreign tongues.

Apartment Laundry

That cute young couple down the hall –
the ones with barely past teenage bodies,
have no idea that every
moan, gasping breath, and
squeaky spring of their
Sunday morning love-making
echoes through the basement
laundry room beneath their bed,
where silver-haired widows,
awash in memories,
turn from each other
with rapid breath,
to add softener to their loads.

Dawn

I lay on my left side,
facing the eastern window
dressed in Italian lace;
the shy sun spreads
his young, pale fingers.

The gods speak to me
in whispers:
We've come!
We're here!
We need your help!

I wake slowly to their call,
the call of my brother birds
my sister deer,
wake to our most precious work:

To love the dawn,
to wrap ourselves in promise,
to pull the sun into the heavens.

Chorus: Age 88

She dreams on pain-free nights
of her dead husband,
young as the day they wed,
standing in mist
 with outstretched arms, calling:
"Come! I have been waiting!"

Some nights they dance
to swing bands
at pre-war clubs in
Windsor and Detroit.
She swears she feels the heat
of his body, long and lean,
wrapped around her in bed.

Nights when her bones
scream and crumble,
she sees her own mother
rattling keys, opening gates,
calling to her daughter:
"Viens, nous t'attendons!"
"Come! We are waiting!"

Three nights this week alone,
she says over pancakes and tea.
"Merde! Je ne suis pas prête!"
"Shit! I am not ready!"

Fishin'

Women learn young to bait their curving hook
with succulence and promise,
trolling for the perfect catch.

With red devil lures dangling from tempting lobes,
they twist and tease in spiked heels,
feet arched like a taut fly-pole.

Fishin' for a snapper, they might reel
in a barracuda. Searchin' for a playful sunfish,
they can catch a mess of crabs.

Women learn to paint flame-red pouty mouths,
shimmy hips on 50-pound test line legs,
tell stories of the great one that got away.

Some take their boats out
and the fish just jump in.
The ones afraid to ply
spinners or brandish a net
buy their fish,
and fry 'em.

Between the Leaves

Don't rake these fallen gold and russet leaves,
let them decompose in autumn rains,
in sleepy garden beds, with memories
you've gathered up since spring.

The time has come for me to leave,
while yellow mums still grace our cobbled path,
before the frigid glance, the frost-cloaked words.
I've never weathered out a rugged winter.

It's April air I love, fresh-scented, sweet
and cool, as we were those first days.
Buds grow to wide-leafed oaks and maples;
handshakes turn to passionate embrace.

We grew love like forget-me-nots,
believing hardy roots hold ever-strong.
Then came the summer solstice of our hearts:
warm air turned chill, sweet petals lost their scent.

Don't rake your fallen god and russet dreams,
but let them decompose in autumn rains
or fallow garden beds, rich food
for love's be-leafing your next spring.

Wallpapering

Measuring our time like lengths of paper,
you fit our interactions to your social plumb line,
insist on perfect seams. You tell me:
a good wallpaper hides a thousand sins.

But I would rather feel the bumps
and indentations of bare plaster
than be tricked by the
symmetry of patterned facades.

I won't stick it out –

You'd want to brush me flat,
a muted rose on your traditional wall.
I'd dance, barefoot
up a makeshift ladder, crying:
Hand me the steamer, Honey,
this paper's coming down.

Cindy Now and Then

Cindy had barely snapped the lid of her Zippo lighter shut when her mother pounded on the bedroom door. "I told you no more smoking in the house, Cindy! Open this door – NOW!"

"Watch this," Cindy whispered to Darla and me. "What's that ma? I can't hear you!" she screamed, as she flung the door open, blew a lungful of smoke into her mother's face, and slammed the door shut again. "Leave us alone, Bitch!" Cindy leaned against the door, took a long drag, and said "Girls, *that's* how you teach your mother who's *really* in charge."

Her mom was still ranting in the next room as the three of us climbed out the window and headed onto the streets.

We had met a few months earlier, when Darla and I walked two miles down the dirt road from our upper-middle-class subdivision to the soda fountain and drug store down by the lake. Darla was reaching for the door when Mr. Wilson, the pharmacist, rushed out, pushing a raven-haired girl in front of him. "Get out and STAY out, you little thief!" he yelled, as he brushed his hands together and walked back into the store. The girl turned to us, shrugged her shoulders and said, "You girls want a cold one on me? Come to my house." Five minutes later, Darla and I had our first taste of beer and cigarettes. We were all of 12 years old.

"I'm just a white trash girl," Cindy said. "This house was my grandparent's summer cottage. Ma ran away when she was 15. She came back preggers with me and conned grandpa into giving her this dump so we'd have a place to live. Now she works at a bar in Walled Lake. I'm 14, I take care of myself, and I take what I want of ma's beer and cigarettes, too." Smoke rings curled around her dark hair.

We went to her house every day after school, learning to draw thick charcoal lines along the edges of our eyelids, purse our lips ever so slightly to emphasize their kissability, and fill our training bras with carefully folded toilet tissue. When summer came, we shyly sunbathed topless in Cindy's back yard because her boyfriend Dale told her tan lines weren't sexy. "Sexy is all we ever need to be," Cindy told us, "They won't tell you that in your snooty Catholic school, girls, but I know all about it, and I guess I'll have to teach you, 'cause no one else will."

When winter came, we giggled through the nun's stuttering explanation of sex, changed out of our plaid school uniforms and into jeans and t-shirts the minute we were home, then ran to sit on Cindy's bed while she flipped through pages of *Hustler* magazine. "Dale told me every girl should look and act like this," she said, staring at a bleached blonde slung naked across a leather couch with her legs akimbo. "He said he could help all three of us be sexy and make a lot more money than if we work at a bar like my ma. He's 18, he should know. So whatcha say? Wanna go out with me and Dale tonight?"

Darla and I were jolted out of our disturbed fascination with the *Hustler* photo. We'd just been invited into Cindy's inner sanctum – a date with Dale and his grown-up friends. Could we tell our mothers we were spending the night at each other's house? Would we get away with sneaking back into Cindy's house after her mother came home from working at the bar? Darla was the first to break. "My mom will know I'm lying," she said, "and besides, I sing in the choir at Sunday mass, so I have to be there early tomorrow." "Yeah me too," I said, my eyes on the floor. "And I forgot – I have to babysit my brother tonight 'cause mom and dad are playing cards with the neighbors. We should probably go home now, Darla."

Two weeks later Darla dragged me into a back corner of the girl's locker room at school. "Yesterday Mr. Wilson at the pharmacy told my mom someone beat Cindy up Saturday night," she whispered. "She's got a black eye and a big bruise on her stomach. My mom says I can't hang out with her anymore. What should we do?"

We told our mothers we were going to the library, skipped west down the street, turned the corner and doubled back to the east, heading for the foot path through the woods that took us cross-country to Cindy's house.

She lay on the sofa, her thick black hair tangled and matted, and her naturally pale skin china-white against the dark red and brown bruise circling her left eye. "It's nothing," she said, "I'm fine. It's just a little bruise, and I deserved it. We were humping in the back seat of his car. When I said he was hurting me, he said if I loved him I'd take whatever he gave. He said I should shut my stupid mouth, and then he punched me, kicked me in the stomach and said I deserved it for ruining his day. It's my own fault – I didn't do what my man wanted. I'm not sexy enough yet. " She spoke matter-of-factly, as if this was a daily occurrence in her life.

Darla and I stayed longer than we dared, pledging our forever friendship with pinkie promises, then headed back to the boring streets of our own neighborhood. We never went back to Cindy's house after that day. Mr. Wilson told Darla's mom that Cindy got pregnant and moved in with Dale, disappearing from our lives as dramatically as she had entered.

But we never forgot her, and with her hesitant entry into the café forty years later, we understood why.

Over the decades, Cindy had become a cult idol, a sweeping legend, to Darla and me. We'd redressed our memories in psychedelic colors, blew her way out of proportion, and made her as important in our pre-teen lives as the Beatles and Rolling Stones. Somehow, despite maturing into women, then mothers, and now matrons, it never occurred to us that Cindy might be anything other than the petite, sassy, chain-smoking brunette with a bloody dagger tattooed on her left breast.

So the frail old woman who hobbled to the back table near the end of the breakfast rush barely caught our attention. She sat quietly, watching the door as I tended to the patrons at nearby tables, and turned her head toward the wall each time the door opened, letting the wide brim of her summer hat shield her profile. "Darla!" she whispered as I came to her table. "Darla! It's me! Cindy! Remember? When we were kids?"

I stared in disbelief at the shocking remains of my childhood friend. "Darla is in the kitchen making scones, Cindy. I'll bring her out in a minute – but first what would you like to eat?"

"I'll have some eggs, Darla," she said, her voice rising to a barely discernible pitch. "Scrambled, with cream cheese and hot sauce... and orange juice, and white toast and *bacon*!" She grabbed my arm as I turned to go, pulled me to her face, and with terror in her eyes, whispered, "Don't tell a soul I'm here, ya hear me?"

"Don't worry, Cindy," I said in a tone these days reserved for my grandchildren. "You're safe here now."

Darla didn't believe me. "No!" she squealed, running to stare through the kitchen door at the odd, aged creature claiming to be our pubescent idol. "Wow. Oh, Wow!" she mouthed over and over, while I quickly prepared Cindy's order.

We delivered the food together. "Oh, Cindy!" Darla said, wearing her widest smile, "Where have you been? You must tell us *everything* that's happened since we last saw you! Here, let me help you with the butter."

Cindy slowly looked up from her plate. Her voice grew fuller and faster with each word. "I've been living abroad for years, girls," she said, waving her hand across her face. "Otherwise, I would have looked you up a long time ago. But you know how it is when you are... traveling."

She turned to the wall, pretending to search through her handbag, as a pair of orderlies from the hospital came through the door. I rose to greet them, catching Darla's eye and her silent, wide-eyed "Oh, Wow!" as I walked past. When the orderlies left with their carry-out orders three minutes later, Cindy turned back to us, the long-ago Zippo lighter in her hand.

"Got a smoke, girlies?" she asked, looking pleadingly from Darla to me. "Sorry, Cindy," Darla said. "It's against the law to smoke in the cafe – and besides, we quit a long time ago. So tell us! Tell us all about your life! We've always wondered…."

"Piss off, Darla!" Cindy hissed, jumping up from her chair as a shadow moved across the front window. "There's no time for foolishness! He's after me… you've got to stop him, the two of you… come on, let's go!" She drug Darla into the kitchen as I turned to the door to welcome three unfamiliar faces.

It's not often strangers come to the café. Cindy's arrival was strange enough, and her frantic run into the kitchen with Darla was both amusing and confusing, but hers was a face from the past. The three men who stepped through the door next were total strangers. The light shifted as they entered; it took me a moment to focus on their faces.

They stood in a triangular formation – the short, squat man in front, the two taller men behind.

"Good morning, Gentlemen! May I suggest the table by the window? It has the best view of the street," I said, directing my speech to the man in front. He said nothing, but motioned to his friends, who took a booth by the door as he followed me to the table. "Nice place you have here, Ma'am," he said as he sat. "I hope you don't mind, but I need a private moment or two with you. It's somewhat urgent."

"Of course," I said, looking him straight in the eye, "Let me grab a fresh pot of coffee for you and your friends, and I'm all yours."

I walked to the kitchen as calmly as I could, Cindy's last statement pounding in my ears. *Is this the man she fears?* Darla and Cindy were huddled in the back corner, Darla's hand firmly over Cindy's mouth. "Take the back route to my house, now!" I whispered, "Stay there until I come or call. And Darla, keep her quiet!"

Had I known the story Cindy would tell Darla, I might have behaved differently that afternoon. But then, the patience to wait for the whole truth has never been part of human nature, has it?

Darla did exactly as I said, gently guiding Cindy out the back door, through the gardens, and into the safety of my home hidden in the trees.

"I've been telling those idiots at the hotel to stop waking me up! I'm just tryin' to sleep, dammit, and they keep coming in, giving me pills, shining lights in my eyes, talking about bruises! Who would want to stay in a hotel like that, Darla?" Cindy said, rolling strands of silk from the scarf between her fingers.

"I wanted to go home and they kept buggin' the shit out of me about my secrets – 'Where'd ya go, Cindy? Aren't you forgetting the bruises, Cindy? Where'd ya hide the money? ' And I'd climb on the table and yell 'It's none of your f-in business!' until they went away. Now I got a big problem – they're after me, and I need to hide out here with you, until I can figure out where to go next. Don't tell them I'm here, or everything will go to shit!"

Over the next five hours, Cindy took Darla down the dark and dangerous streets of her life. She'd moved in with Dale when she became pregnant all those years ago, and was told after two days of hard labor that her child had died. When she was released from the hospital, she found her apartment empty. Dale had disappeared.

A year later she was dancing in Vegas when she met a handsome Spaniard who romanced her from one end of the Pyrenees to the other, leaving her alone and penniless on a dirt road outside of Barcelona. Next it was an almost-royal Brit, who would have been a Duke had his bloodlines only been a bit more palatable, then the Aussie tour guide who blackened her eye and robbed her of her meager barmaid earnings.

"Seems it takes a hard knock or two to get things through my skull!" she said, scooping a second helping of shepherd's pie on her plate. "I'll tell ya what I've learned, Darla! Never trust a man! NEVER! It don't matter if they're rich or poor, smart or dumb, they just lie and treat ya for shit."

Somewhere along the line, and without explanation, Cindy found herself serving thick black coffee and grits at an Alabama truck stop. "That's when the real trouble started," she told Darla as they washed the dinner dishes. "That's when that chubby one with the mean eyes showed up and started calling me 'ma.' There's something wrong with that one! Bruise! Bruise! I tell you he's dangerous and bat-shit crazy!"

Cindy grabbed the last of the steak knives Darla was washing and held it to her own neck. "Don't you tell him I'm here, Darla, or I'll have to quiet you by force! They're after me, and now they're after you, too because that crazy bastard heard me tell the hotel nurse I was hoping to find you. Then the crazy ass told me I would never find anyone until I told him what he wanted to know. Bruise! Bruise! I told him to eat shit and slammed the hotel door in his face. I watched through the window until the miserable bastard left, and then I told the hotel staff I was going for a little stroll down the hall. I just kept walking once I got out the door, and here I am – no shit!"

"My lips are sealed, Cindy, and, you're safe here. Let's put the last of the dishes away, shall we?" Darla said, slipping the knife out of Cindy's hand. "Come, there is a soft bed waiting for you in the other room. I'm sure you must be tired after such a busy day."

"Oh, my, yes!" Cindy said, slipping into the bed. "Please wake me at 8, and tell the cook I'll have pancakes for breakfast." Five minutes later, satisfied that Cindy was sound asleep, Darla picked up the phone to call Sheriff Bailey.

I'd barely poured the first round of coffee for the three strangers when the back door slammed and Brent the busboy bounced into the café for the lunch shift. "Brent!" I said before my guests had a chance to open their mouths, "Please go tell Mr. Bailey his lunch has been delayed."

Brent took a step back, said, "You got it, ma'am," spun on his heel and was out the back door in five strides. "Mr. Bailey's lunch" was a café code we dreamed up years ago to indicate trouble; Brent ran the two blocks to Sheriff Bailey's office while I waited for the strangers to show their hand.

"My name is Bruce Meadows," the short man said, "and I believe you know my mother – one Cindy Simmons."

"I did indeed know a Cindy Simmons," I said calmly, "But that was many years ago, when I was just a girl."

"You've seen her recently?"

"It's been decades since Cindy lived in this area," I said, matching his intense stare. "What could possibly bring her back?"

"You. She's looking for you. Seems you might have the answers she won't give me herself."

"Look, Mr. Meadows, I'm always willing to help a friend. Why don't you tell me what this is all about and why you think Cindy would come here?"

"Fair enough, but first call off the cops…yeah, I saw the look in the kid's eye and figured you'd given him some sort of warning," He said. "You have nothing to fear from me. Here's my card."

"Bruce Meadows, PhD—Social Worker/Author" the card said. *He said she was his mother*, I thought. *What the hell is going on?*

"My mother took off when I was twelve," he said. "My dad was gone long before that. I grew up in a string of foster homes in tough neighborhoods, and eventually landed in state prison for armed robbery. The prison chaplain took me under his wing and with his help, by the time I was released, I had completed high school and a year of college. I moved in with his family, married his daughter, and eventually finished several degrees.

"Years went by and I was quite happy with my life. Then one day about four years ago, I got a call from University Hospital, saying my mother had been admitted and I needed to sign some papers. You can imagine my surprise. She'd been out of my life for so long I had almost forgotten about her. But there she was, and in my first look at her face, everything came rushing back — the drugs, the alcohol, the endless string of abusive men that came through our house. She was worn and haggard and clearly insane, but I still saw the young face I remember from when I was a boy. I loved her. I hated her."

"She had been run down on the street — apparently she's been living on the streets for years. The doctors found a photo of the two of us in her bra, from when I was five years old, and my name was printed on the back. Can you believe that? All these years! The hospital Googled my name and, well, I'm sort of famous from a few books I've written, so it wasn't hard for them to find me.

"She's totally insane. She thinks I'm a dangerous man, out to kill her or something. I put her in a nice nursing home near my office on the west side of the state, and the next thing I know, she's convinced them to let her go outside, and wandered off, two weeks ago. Fortunately, she said something to the nurse about coming to find you. She's old and frail and batty as hell and needs round-the-clock care. I'm exhausted from trying to keep up with my business while I've been hunting for her – and you – for two weeks. So here I am, hoping for your help. Have you seen my mother?"

The back door slammed; Bruce flinched as Brent bounded into the cafe, followed by his father, Sheriff Randall Bailey, and Walker Pith, his deputy.

"Good Afternoon, Sheriff!" I said, meeting them near the center of the café. "I'm so sorry about your lunch! You must think I'm losing it!"

"Perhaps we should talk again later?" Bruce said, moving to the door. "I'll come back tomorrow around 3:00?"

"Yes, I suppose that would be fine," I said, "thank you for stopping by."

I stood with the Sheriff, the deputy, and Brent while the three men left the cafe, slipping into a black Mercedes parked at the corner.

"What the heck is going on here?" Sheriff Bailey asked. "I thought you were in trouble, especially after Darla called and told me about these characters."

"So did I, Randall," I said, taking his hand as we walked into the kitchen. "I sent Brent for you before I heard that man's story. Nothing's happened, but I'm not convinced everything is alright, so I'm keeping my cards close to my vest. Meanwhile there is an old lady at my house who needs care, and we have to keep her from getting away from us tonight. Think you could keep an eye out overnight?"

"Sure thing," the Sheriff said, giving me a quick peck on the cheek. "Long as you feed me! I'll meet you there at 6:00."

The rest of the day was status quo; I cooked during the lulls, and interacted with customers during peak hours. Brent took over seating people in addition to bussing the tables, since Darla was tending to Cindy. I'd pretty much forgotten the odd events of the morning by the time I closed for the day and headed home to watch the evening news.

"The FBI has issued a warning to all persons in SE Michigan: a dangerous criminal has escaped from federal prison and is suspected to be in the area. More after weather and traffic," the news anchor said with a smile that belied the gravity of the story she had just reported.

Sheriff Randall and I were cuddled on the sofa, sharing crusty Tuscan bread and a shrimp fondue with Darla.

"Hhmm – I'm surprised I haven't heard anything," he said. "Unless this is fresh breaking..." He said, just as the cell phone clipped to his belt – the one he never turned off, even when we were in bed together – sent off the official police business signal. "Damn, girl! I've got to go, but I'll be back to check in on you!"

I'd grown accustomed to dates cut short when police situations arose, and always had a "Plan B." Darla had just filled us in on Cindy's story, and I'd told her about the interaction with Bruce, why I didn't let on that she was at my home, and my sense that the whole truth had not been told. We had to decide what to do in the morning.

"The FBI and local law enforcement officers are on the lookout for Bruce Pfeffer, a dangerous criminal who escaped from a federal prison facility two weeks ago and is believed to be in the area," the news anchor said. A picture of Bruce Meadows flashed on the screen. Darla and I sat bolt upright, Tuscan bread halfway to our mouths, staring at the screen.

"Mr. Pfeffer was serving a life sentence," the reporter continued. "Twenty years ago, he and his parents – Dale and Cindy Pfeffer – robbed a bank in Brownsville, Texas. Two officers and the senior Mr. Pfeffer were killed that day, all with bullets from Bruce Pfeffer's gun. Mrs. Pfeffer, who grew up in southeast Michigan, and the 1.5 million dollars she escaped with, were never found."

And there she was on the TV screen – a grainy bank surveillance photo of the 30-something Cindy, looking pretty much like we remembered her, but wielding a machine gun as she ran from the bank, a satchel of money slung over her shoulder.

"Pfeffer is believed to be accompanied by several other inmates who escaped with him." Mug shots of the two men who came into the café that morning flashed on the screen.

"Police suspect they are attempting to find Mrs. Pfeffer. They are believed to be armed and dangerous. Should you see any of these men, contact your local police department immediately. In what could be a related story, a black Mercedes was reported stolen in Toledo late last night, by three armed men who match the suspect's description. More on that in our update at 11:00. Now here's Paulette with the channel lineup for tonight."

"Oh, WOW!" Darla said, jumping from the sofa and heading over to close the door to the hallway the hallway that lead to the room in which Cindy was sleeping. "I knew she was a bit off her rocker, but... *a bank robber?* Oh, wow! Oh....*What?*" she screamed and ducked as the living room window shattered.

I flipped over the sofa, too, landing right next to her on the floor, while guns roared and bullets ripped into the walls. Perhaps it lasted two minutes; it felt like hours. Darla and I clung to each other long after the gunshots stopped.

"What the hell?" Darla whispered. "Are we safe, or about to be dead?"

"I don't know," I whispered back. "But I guess there's only one way to find out. We've got to stand up and look outside."

"Oh, WOW! Oh, No!" Darla said. "Let's sit a few minutes longer."

Footsteps crunched on broken glass outside the door. We held our breaths as the door creaked open. I peeked around the corner of the sofa, and recognized the worn old sneakers Randall wore the minute he was off duty.

"Randall!" I yelled, jumping right over the sofa and into his arms. "What the hell?"

"There's three dead thugs in your front yard... no, you don't need to be lookin' now. Bruce Pfeffer and his boys are dead. The coroner is on his way, and so are the FBI. They're mighty interested in talking to your guest Cindy."

"Oh my God, Cindy!" Darla cried, heading toward the hallway.

"No! Darla! Don't go there," Randall said.

"But, someone has to tell…." Darla said, taking another step toward the door.

"Darla! I'm the Sheriff, and I'm tellin' you to *stop*… right now!"

Randall shooed us into the kitchen as the FBI agents stepped through the door, and pointed them towards the hallway.

"Clear!" the first agent yelled at the door of my room, and "Clear!" at the door of the next room, unoccupied. The third room was where Darla had left Cindy.

We heard the door open, heard the agent yell, "Stay where you are! Hands above your Head!" A heavy silence followed.

We stood in the kitchen, Darla clinging to me, and me clinging to Randall, until the FBI captain came in.

"She's gone," he said. "Bedroom window wide open. Musta been a while ago, since she wasn't with the men outside."

Randall followed him into the hallway. I went to my room to pack an overnight bag; finding a letter from Cindy tucked in my lingerie drawer. I slipped it in my bag and read it to Darla an hour later, when we were alone in the small apartment above the cafe.

By the time you realize I've gone, I'll be halfway around the world with a new look, a new name, and a new life. The story the police will eventually tell you is true, but it's not the whole truth. Bruce is my son, and he's even meaner and more dangerous than his father.

Cindy's bare knees crashed into the icy snow. The black plastic garbage bag holding her clothes slid across the yard. She grabbed her stomach and retched. Scooping snow to wipe the vomit from her face, she retrieved the bag, walked twenty paces to the street, and suck out her thumb. Hours later, two palm-print bruises would form over her shoulder blades, visual reminders of the force her mother had used in pushing her out the door for the last time.

"Crazy Bitch," she said to Dale as he handed her another cold beer later that night. "I come home pregnant just like her – does she help me the way her folks did?"

Yes, I was involved in the bank heist. And yes, I got away with the money. I got out while the shooting was still going on, ran through back alleys for four blocks. Two hours later I strolled out of an underground tunnel into Mexico, free as a bird. That was the plan all along – to get the cash, get to Mexico, and never look back.

Cindy's lungs burned; she'd never run ten feet much less four city blocks worth of trash-strewn alleyways with a huge, heavy sack on her back, but adrenalin blasted through her veins and somehow, she made it to the old house whose dirt basement walls hid the escape tunnel entrance. The three-story building had been empty for years, but the taxes were paid, and the working-class neighbors rarely saw the drug runners coming in and out. She'd dropped the machine gun right outside the bank entrance, and stuffed the surgical gloves that kept her fingerprints from linking her forensically to the weapon into her pockets as she ran. The handgun Dale insisted she wear was still safely attached to the inner waistband of her jeans.

Still hearing the sirens and shouts from the bank, she reached for the front door latch and exhaled deeply when the door opened easily. *This must have been an elegant home a long time ago,* she thought, noticing the turn-of-the-century architectural details as she strode down the hall to the kitchen, where a steep flight of wooden steps led her to the basement. *Wish I had time to enjoy it.* Cindy took the steps two at a time and found the empty bookcase that concealed the tunnel's entry. She lifted the left edge of the second shelf, revealing a small latch which, when tripped, caused the entire bookshelf to slide to the left. She stepped through the doorway, hit the second latch just inside, and took a deep breath as the bookshelf slid back into place and the dim lights strung along the tunnel turned on.

61

Cindy dropped the money sack, and reached inside the duffel bag Dale had stashed in the tunnel a week earlier. Bruce had put the entire escape plan together – disguises, routes, even the money laundering connections. She grabbed her change of clothes and disguises, hoisted the money sack onto her back, and headed into the hand-hewed tunnel. The dimly lit path was a fairly rapid decline of almost a half mile, where it connected with an old, unused train tunnel under the Rio Grande, then rose again along the same distance at the other end. Two hours after entering the old home in Brownsville, she emerged into the basement of a carefully groomed boarding house located two miles south in Matamoros, Mexico.

Twenty minutes later, she walked to the front door wearing a black business suit over a crisp while blouse, three-inch open-toed heels, a chin-length strawberry blond wig, and carrying a designer product sample case full of beauty products. One and half million dollars were in the wheeled suitcase she pulled. No one would see anything unusual about the businesswoman who spent a restful night in the boarding house.

Dale and Bruce were dead; there was neither time nor reason to feel remorse. She must continue with the plan for her own survival. Cindy locked eyes and nodded to the local man in the front hall easy chair. Minutes later, she was in a beat-up taxi, on her way to the back offices of a small manufacturing facility some forty miles further into the Mexican countryside. She was on her own for the first time in her life. The further she walked in those three-inch heels, the wider her smile grew.

Can you understand how I felt? Free for the first time in my life, and with more money than I could ever imagine. I took the shootout as my chance for freedom. Freedom from Dale and Bruce, freedom from the law, freedom to make whatever kind of life I wanted. I bargained some of the money away, just to get the rest laundered and a new identity, and then I went to Europe. I went from one country to another, one town to another, changing identities every six months.

England and Ireland were easy enough as there was no language barrier, and no social barrier that money couldn't overcome. She reminded herself each morning of her name and concocted history, remained aloof from those she employed, and even more distant from those with whom she socialized as a matter of blending into the local culture.

In England she feigned engagement with an Italian stonemason; in Ireland, with a Croatian shop owner. She became a smiling face in the villages in which she lived, and a resource to all from whom she accepted employment. No matter where she settled, she settled quickly and became an instant member of the community, learning the local dialect and blending in so thoroughly no one would ever think her time there had been short.

But her eyes were always looking behind, watching for the watcher, waiting for the moment of exposure. From Ireland, she crossed the channel and made her way to Portugal, then France, then Spain.

After five years I figured my trail was adequately cold, so I bought a small Spanish villa and hired a tutor, learning proper Spanish, and proper English as well. In short, girls, over time I made myself into a respectable woman, just like the two of you. I lived quietly and simply, working in small offices, keeping the money safe, and feeling good about myself.

Until the day the letter came.

It was an ordinary envelope, addressed in English to "The Lady of the House" and bore a Texas, USA postmark. I can't tell you how the shadows fell across my door and my heart when I saw that. It was from Bruce, from his prison cell in Texas. How he tracked me down he didn't say, but he rambled on about my having to pay for my "sins" and made vague threats. I had settled down, but kept the connections that made it possible for a quick get-away. That afternoon, I emptied my bank accounts and with one phone call to an old friend, walked away from the life I had lived for so many years with yet another fake identity, and a Hollywood-style makeover into a decrepit old woman.

I knew it was only a matter of time before he found me again; I had to take matters into my own hands to save myself. So I responded to his letter. I told him how grateful I was for his actions all those years ago – he saved my life by being the monster he is. I told him there was a half million dollars in a safe deposit box in Michigan; I was on my way to empty it out. I told him he could rot in hell for all I cared.

The only way I could eliminate the threat he posed was to draw him out, and he responded exactly as I thought he would – escaping from prison to come after me.

He'd heard your names; I talked about you when he was a little thing. So I suppose it was easy enough for him to ask around and find you, since neither of you had gone far. Playing the crazy old lady was sort of fun, and the two of you were so quick to accept that I was a frail old lunatic! It was amusing and depressing at the same time.

And now I've led him right into the trap I've set. I've led him and the law enforcement people on his tail right to your door. That's not exactly what I intended – into your home, I mean, but in the end it had to be this way. Hopefully they'll blow his brains out so he'll never find me again. Neither will anyone else.

Thanks for the food and the bed.

Cindy

A small key marked "1ˢᵗ National Bank and Trust" fell from the envelope. "Oh, Wow!" was all Darla could say.

About The Author

Linda Angér is the owner of The Write Concept, Inc., a marketing communications company founded in 2000. Her clients have included DaimlerChrysler Corporation, Valeo Corporation, The Crittenton Hospital Medical Center Foundation, HAVEN, The Royal Park Hotel, Golson Book Design (NYC), Whole Bubble Thinking (Brisbane, Australia), and hundreds of small businesses throughout Michigan. Her business writing has been featured in *Black Engineer Magazine, Profiles in Diversity Journal, MultiCultural Law Journal,* and in many online business magazines. Her poetry and short stories have appeared in national publications such as *Mused-the Bella Online Journal, Still Crazy Magazine,* and the *Almost Touching* Anthology. She is an avid member of Toastmasters International, and loves coaching other writers to become great speakers.

Linda lives and works in Rochester Hills, Michigan.